Step Up Kids

WorkBook

Subtraction

DreamTivity

Count and Cross Out

Count the objects. Write the number in each box.

Count how many  .

Count how many are crossed out.

—

Now count how many are left.

Count how many  .

Count how many are crossed out.

—

Count how many are left.

StepUp Kids WORKBOOK　　2　　SUBTRACTION

Count how many in all.
How many are crossed out? How many are left?

4 − 1 = 3

In all — Crossed out = What's left

☐ − ☐ = ☐

In all — Crossed out = What's left

☐ − ☐ = ☐

In all — Crossed out = What's left

☐ − ☐ = ☐

In all — Crossed out = What's left

StepUp Kids WORKBOOK — 3 — SUBTRACTION

Subtracting Things

When you subtract, the answer is called the **difference**. Subtract and write the differences.

3 − 1 =

5 − 1 =

5 − 2 =

8 − 4 =

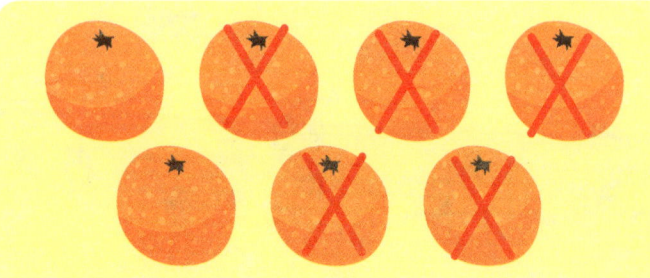

7 − 5 =

StepUp Kids WORKBOOK — SUBTRACTION

Cross out objects to subtract each number. Write the difference in each box.

4 − 2 =

6 − 2 =

8 − 3 =

9 − 5 =

7 − 3 =

StepUp Kids WORKBOOK   SUBTRACTION

Subtracting Things

Cross out objects to subtract the correct number. Write the difference in each box.

3 − 1 = 2

4 − 2 =

2 − 0 =

3 − 2 =

4 − 1 =

3 − 1 =

4 − 3 =

1 − 1 =

2 − 1 =

Subtract and write each difference.

9 − 5 = ☐

7 − 3 = ☐

5 − 2 = ☐

8 − 3 = ☐

6 − 4 = ☐

Think. Think. Think!

Challenge! How many must you subtract to get each difference?

 7 − ☐ = 5

 10 − ☐ = 3

 8 − ☐ = 4

 9 − ☐ = 5

10 − ☐ = 4

Stacked Subtraction

$$\begin{array}{r}5\\-2\\\hline 3\end{array}$$

Cross out to subtract. Write the differences.

$$\begin{array}{r}3\\-1\\\hline\end{array}$$

$$\begin{array}{r}5\\-3\\\hline\end{array}$$

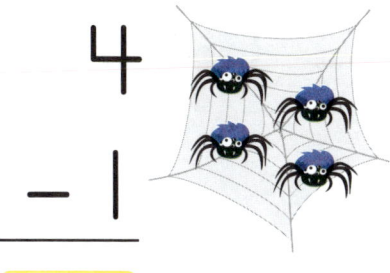

$$\begin{array}{r}4\\-1\\\hline\end{array}$$

$$\begin{array}{r}4\\-3\\\hline\end{array}$$

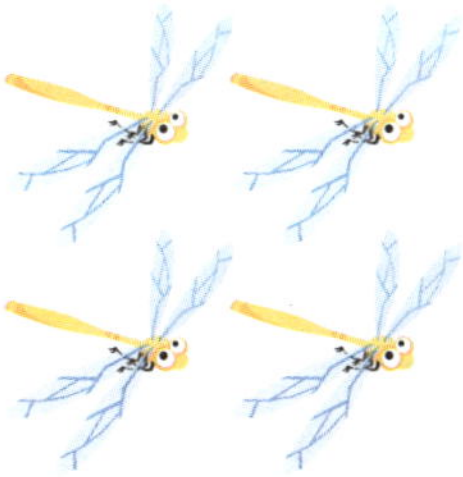

$$\begin{array}{r}5\\-1\\\hline\end{array}$$

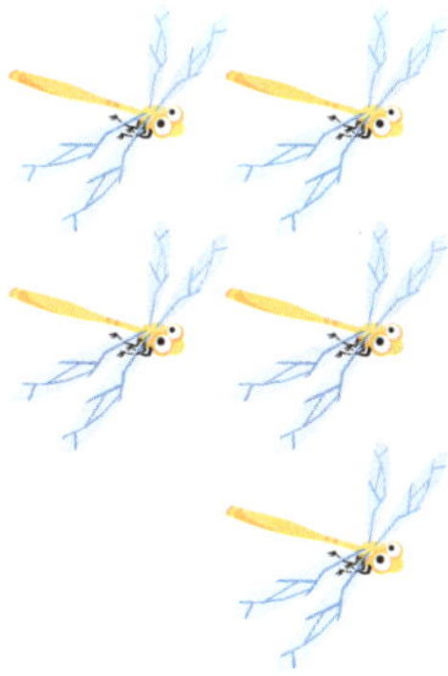

$$\begin{array}{r}2\\-1\\\hline\end{array}$$

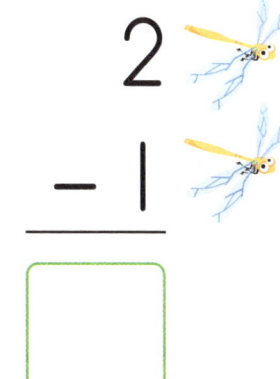

$$\begin{array}{r}4\\-2\\\hline\end{array}$$

$$\begin{array}{r}3\\-2\\\hline\end{array}$$

$$\begin{array}{r}5\\-4\\\hline\end{array}$$

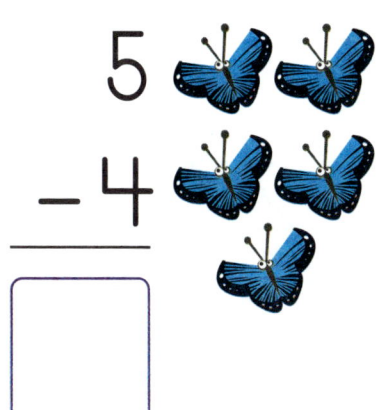

Subtraction Practice

Cross out to subtract. Write the differences.

8
− 3

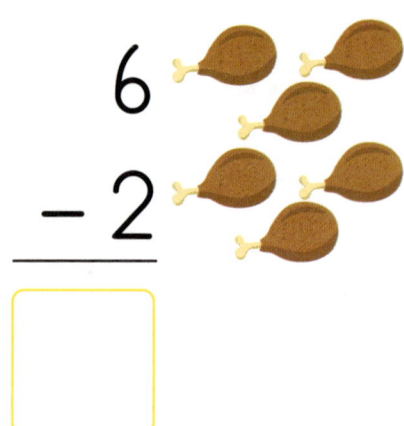

5
− 3

6
− 2

4
− 1

6
− 4

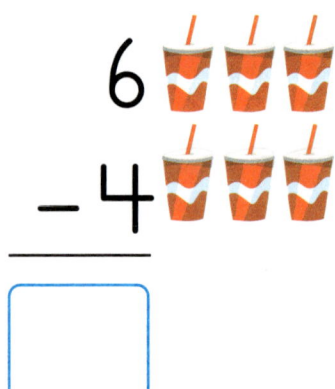

2
− 1

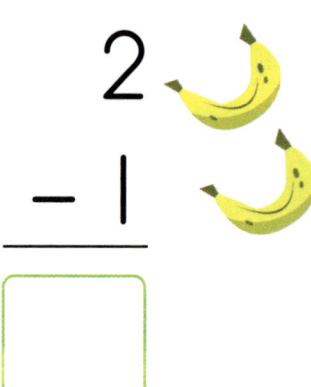

3
− 2

6
− 1

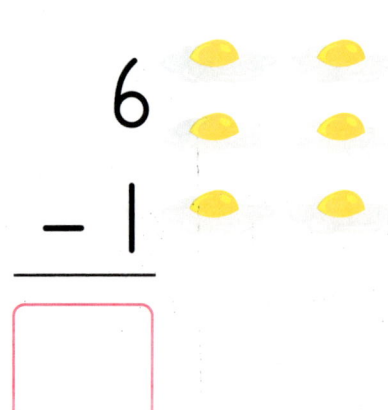

7
− 5

StepUp Kids WORKBOOK   SUBTRACTION

Cross out to subtract. Write the differences.

6 − 3 =

5 − 4 =

7 − 3 =

8 − 2 =

3 − 1 =

5 − 2 =

4 − 2 =

8 − 5 =

4 − 3 =

Subtract Using a Number Line

$$5 - 3 = 2$$

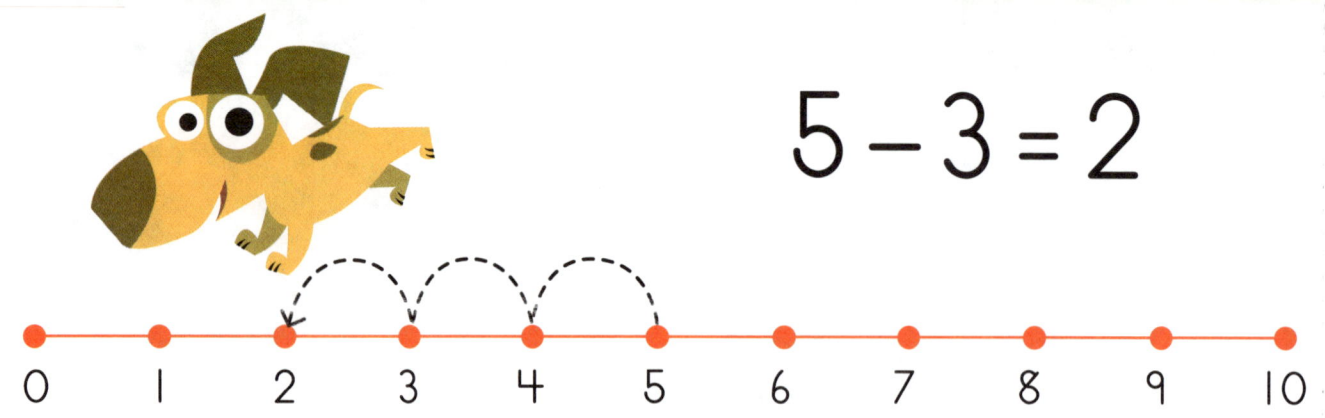

Use the number line to subtract and find each difference.

0 1 2 3 4 5

$4 - 2 =$ ☐

0 1 2 3 4 5

$1 - 0 =$ ☐

0 1 2 3 4 5

$5 - 4 =$ ☐

0 1 2 3 4 5

$3 - 1 =$ ☐

0 1 2 3 4 5

$4 - 3 =$ ☐

0 1 2 3 4 5

$5 - 2 =$ ☐

0 1 2 3 4 5

$3 - 2 =$ ☐

0 1 2 3 4 5

$2 - 2 =$ ☐

Use the number line to subtract and find each difference.

0 1 2 3 4 5 6 7 8 9 10

3 − 2 = ☐   5 − 3 = ☐   5 − 1 = ☐

1 − 1 = ☐   4 − 3 = ☐   2 − 1 = ☐

0 1 2 3 4 5 6 7 8 9 10

```
  4       3       4       2       3
 -2      -1      -4      -0      -3
 ──      ──      ──      ──      ──
 ☐       ☐       ☐       ☐       ☐

 10       9       8      10       7
 -4      -2      -4      -5      -5
 ──      ──      ──      ──      ──
 ☐       ☐       ☐       ☐       ☐
```

StepUp Kids WORKBOOK — SUBTRACTION

Subtract Using a Number Line

0 1 2 3 4 5 6 7 8 9 10 11 12 13 14 15 16 17 18 19 20

| 17
−5 | 12
−3 | 14
−4 | 18
−9 | 13
−7 |

| 15
−3 | 10
−1 | 13
−2 | 20
−3 | 18
−4 |

| 16
−5 | 9
−6 | 19
−4 | 11
−3 | 13
−5 |

| 17
−3 | 18
−6 | 12
−5 | 14
−7 | 16
−7 |

Petal Problems

Subtract the outer number from the center number of the flower. Write the answer on each outside petal.

StepUp Kids WORKBOOK   15   SUBTRACTION

Challenge!

What number must you subtract from to get each difference?

☐ − 1 = 1	☐ − 2 = 3
☐ − 4 = 5	☐ − 3 = 1
☐ − 6 = 4	☐ − 2 = 7
☐ − 5 = 3	☐ − 6 = 6
☐ − 1 = 6	☐ − 5 = 5
☐ − 3 = 4	☐ − 2 = 4
☐ − 3 = 6	☐ − 6 = 1

Bubble Riddles

Write each missing number to complete each equation.

N	E	T
11	_	9
−6	−1	−7
—	—	—
5	2	2

O	W	G	S	L	P
10	5	12	_	8	_
−_	−4	−_	−1	−_	−5
—	—	—	—	—	—
4	5	5	8	4	3

Match your answers with the letters to solve the riddles.

What is full of holes but still holds water?

S	P	O	N	G	E
9	8	6	5	7	3

What gets wetter the more it dries?

T	O	W	E	L
2	6	1	3	4

Practice!

Subtract and write the differences.

2 − 1 =

8 − 4 =

6 − 1 =   5 − 2 =   7 − 5 =

5 − 3 =   8 − 7 =   3 − 1 =

8 − 5 =   9 − 4 =   5 − 4 =

8 − 6 =   7 − 7 =   7 − 4 =

3 − 2 =   6 − 3 =   9 − 1 =

7 − 3 =   9 − 2 =   4 − 3 =

Subtract and write the differences.

```
  6      4      3
 -5     -2     -2
 ___    ___    ___
 [ ]    [ ]    [ ]

 12     10     10     10     10
 -2     -7     -5     -6     -3
 ___    ___    ___    ___    ___
 [ ]    [ ]    [ ]    [ ]    [ ]

  6      8      7      8      7
 -2     -8     -2     -3     -1
 ___    ___    ___    ___    ___
 [ ]    [ ]    [ ]    [ ]    [ ]

  9      7      5      9      6
 -3     -6     -1     -3     -4
 ___    ___    ___    ___    ___
 [ ]    [ ]    [ ]    [ ]    [ ]
```

We're a Family!

A fact family is a group of math facts, or equations, that use the same set of three numbers. There are four addition and subtraction equations that use the same three numbers. These are a fact family!

Example:

These numbers can create these four equations in a fact family:

$4 + 5 = 9$
$5 + 4 = 9$
$9 - 5 = 4$
$9 - 4 = 5$

Complete each family of facts.

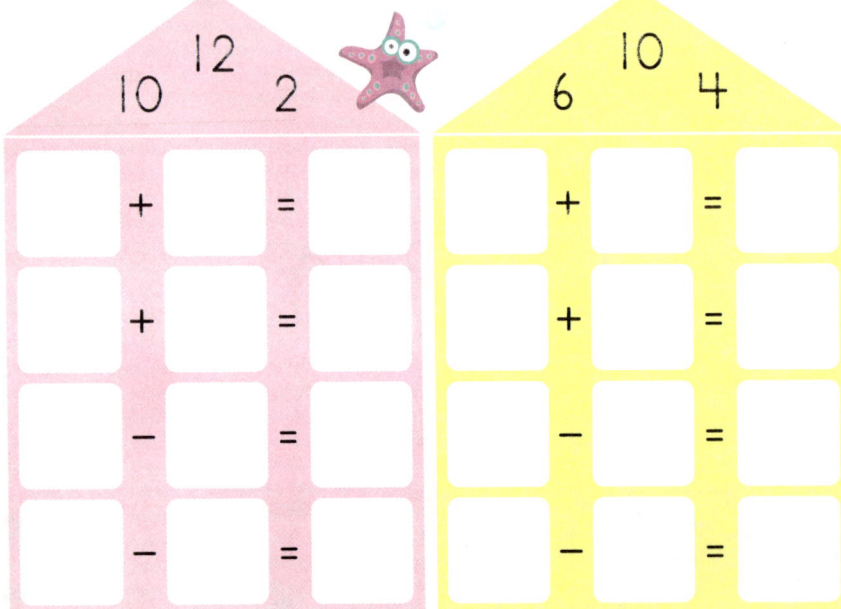

10 12 2

6 10 4

4 7 3

Fact Families

Complete each family of facts.

Challenge!

Solve each equation.
Watch the signs! Some are subtraction and some are addition!

```
  12        3        9        8        4
 - 3       + 2      - 1      - 2      + 2
```

```
   7       12       10        2        5
 + 4      - 1      + 5      + 6      - 1
```

```
   5        6        9        7        4
 - 2      - 5      - 2      - 2      + 1
```

StepUp Kids WORKBOOK — SUBTRACTION

Watch the Signs!

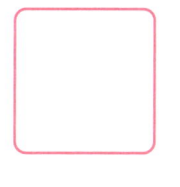

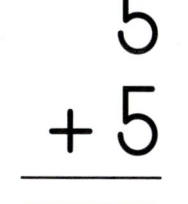

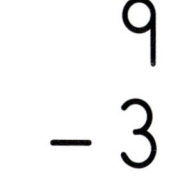

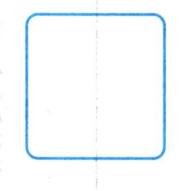

6	10	7	9	12
−4	−3	+0	−6	−6

5	3	8	9	10
+4	+5	−3	−7	+3

9	6	5	9	8
+2	−3	+5	−3	−6

6	7	9	10	6
+4	−3	−4	+2	+6

Challenge! Subtracting Ones and Tens

Subtract the **ones**. Then subtract the **tens**.

Write each difference.

```
 43      58      63      45      63
-12     -24     -42     -34     -52
___     ___     ___     ___     ___
```

```
 47      72      89      87      76
-23     -12     -86     -61     -13
___     ___     ___     ___     ___
```

24

$$\begin{array}{r}\text{TENS ONES}\\26\\-13\\\hline 13\end{array}$$

Subtract the ones. Then subtract the tens. What is the difference?

$$\begin{array}{r}12\\-10\\\hline\end{array}\qquad\begin{array}{r}23\\-11\\\hline\end{array}\qquad\begin{array}{r}18\\-12\\\hline\end{array}\qquad\begin{array}{r}36\\-13\\\hline\end{array}\qquad\begin{array}{r}43\\-22\\\hline\end{array}$$

$$\begin{array}{r}77\\-44\\\hline\end{array}\qquad\begin{array}{r}28\\-11\\\hline\end{array}\qquad\begin{array}{r}37\\-15\\\hline\end{array}\qquad\begin{array}{r}44\\-23\\\hline\end{array}\qquad\begin{array}{r}89\\-57\\\hline\end{array}$$

$$\begin{array}{r}93\\-21\\\hline\end{array}\qquad\begin{array}{r}26\\-14\\\hline\end{array}\qquad\begin{array}{r}34\\-21\\\hline\end{array}\qquad\begin{array}{r}65\\-32\\\hline\end{array}\qquad\begin{array}{r}57\\-31\\\hline\end{array}$$

Story Problems

Read each story problem. (It's okay if an adult helps with the reading.) Will you need to use addition or subtraction to find the answer? Solve and write your answer.

Problem	Answer
Tom wants to make a total of 12 goals in a 2-day soccer tournament. On Friday he made 7 goals. How many goals does he need to make on Saturday?	12 − 7 = ?	5 Goals
Naomi lost 23 golf balls last year. This year she lost only 15. How many has she lost in all?	Problem	Answer Balls
Mateo opened up a case of 48 tennis balls. He handed out most of the balls to his teammates and kept the remaining 12 for himself. How many did he hand out?	Problem	Answer Balls
Emma had 28 baseball caps. She gave 6 to her little sister. How many does Emma have left?  	Problem	Answer Caps
Ben, Elijah, and Alfred are on the same baseball team. In one game, Ben scored 2 runs, Elijah scored 3, and Alfred scored 4. Together, how many runs did they score?	Problem	Answer Runs

StepUp Kids WORKBOOK — SUBTRACTION

Problem	Answer
Jack and Ethan played one-on-one basketball. Jack scored 22 baskets. Ethan scored 34. How many more baskets did Ethan score than Jack?	Baskets
Mia and Molly are on the swim team. Molly swam her race in 58 seconds. Mia beat Molly's time by 4 seconds. What was Mia's race time?	Seconds
Owen, Kelley, and Avery went bowling. In the first frame, Owen knocked down 9 pins, Kelley knocked down 7, and Avery knocked down 4. How many did they knock down in all?	Pins
In the ice skating competition, Zoey performed her best ever! When she finished, people threw 17 pink teddy bears onto the ice for her. Other people threw 12 blue teddy bears. How many teddy bears did she collect from the ice?	Teddy Bears
The neighborhood kids want to play softball. They need to have 9 kids on each of the two teams. So far, 13 kids want to play. How many more players do they need?	Players

Answers

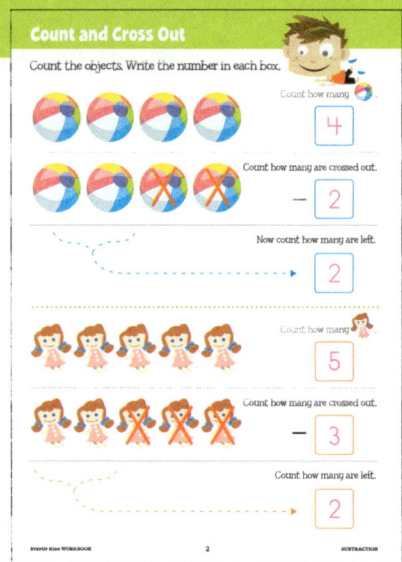
page 2

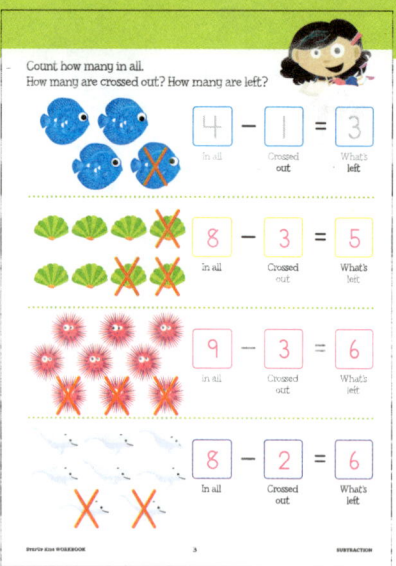
page 3

page 4

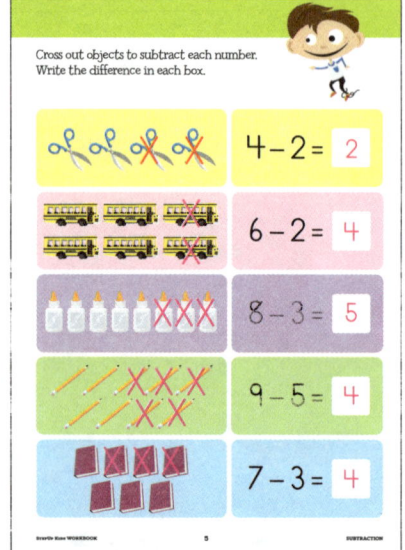
page 5

page 6

page 7

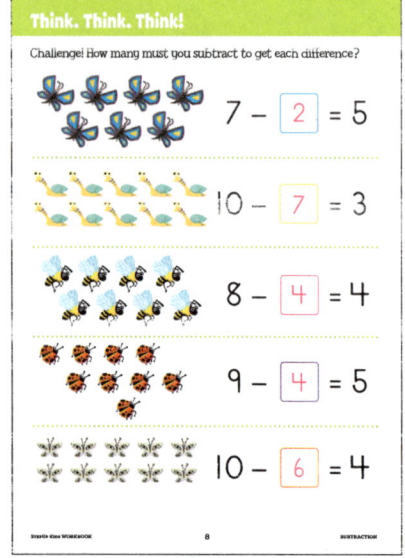
page 8

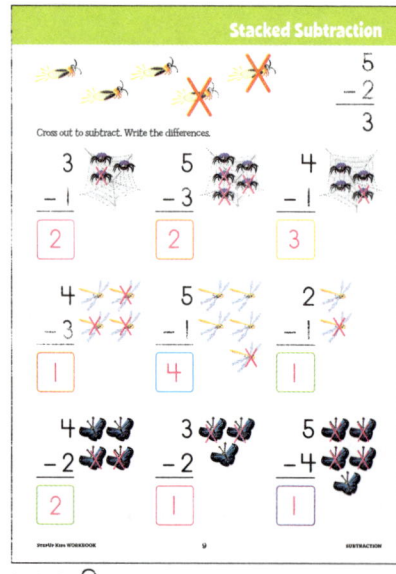
page 9

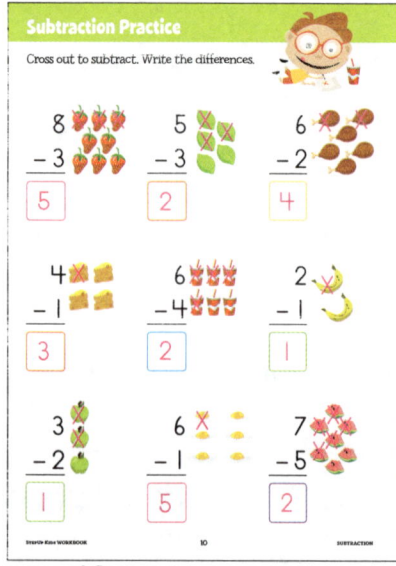
page 10

Answers

page 11

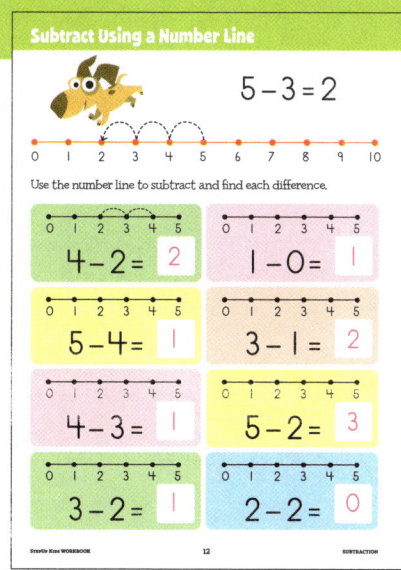
page 12

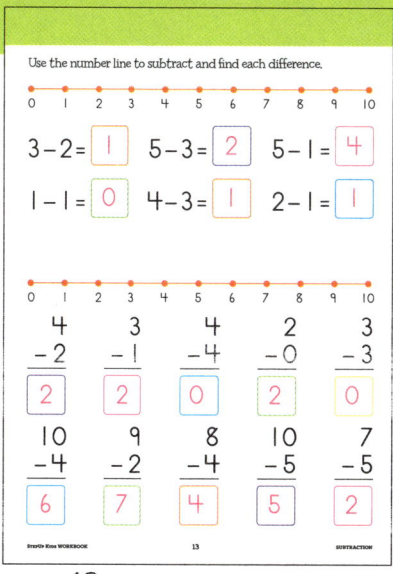
page 13

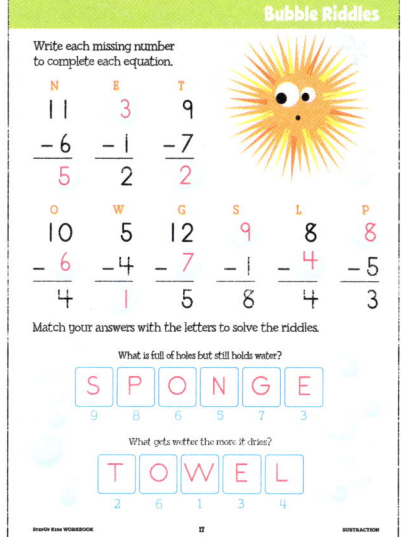
page 14

page 15

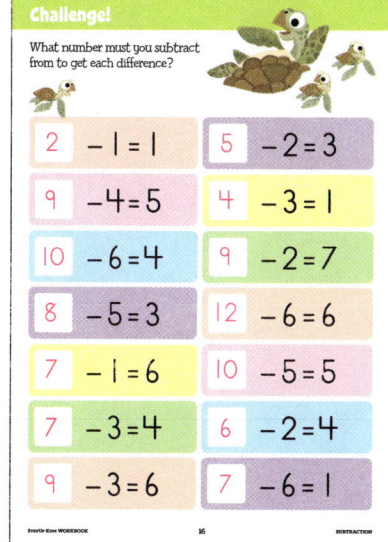
page 16

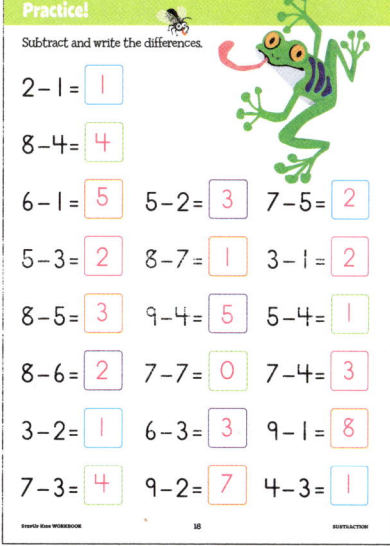
page 17

page 18

page 19

StepUp Kids WORKBOOK 29 SUBTRACTION

Answers

page 20

page 21

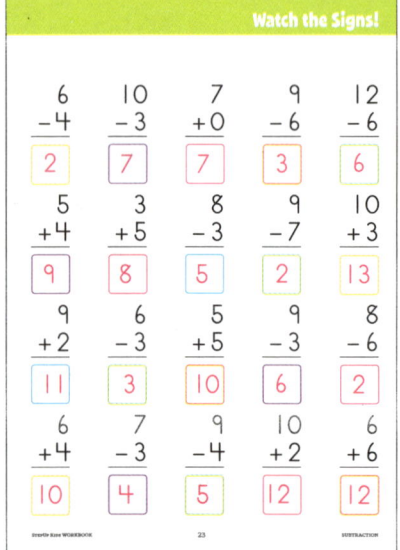

page 23

page 24

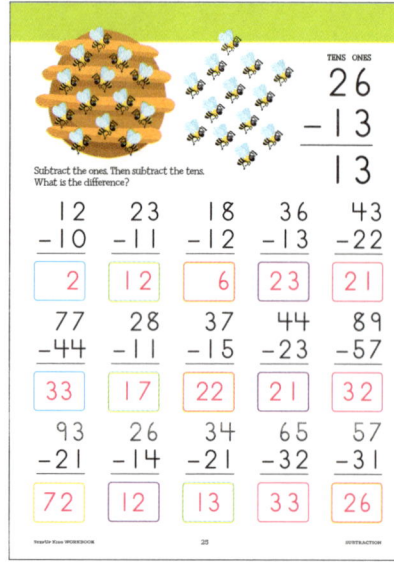

page 25

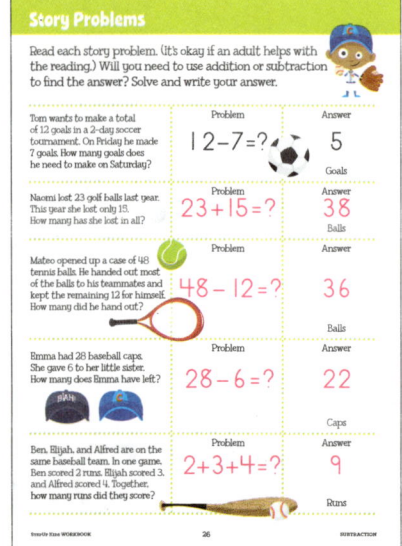

page 26

Subtraction Flash Cards

Carefully cut out to practice and learn subtraction facts. To check your answer, turn the card over to see the answer in the corner box.

→

10 −5 ───	10 −6 ───	10 −3 ───
9 −4 ───	9 −2 ───	8 −5 ───
8 −8 ───	7 −1 ───	7 −3 ───

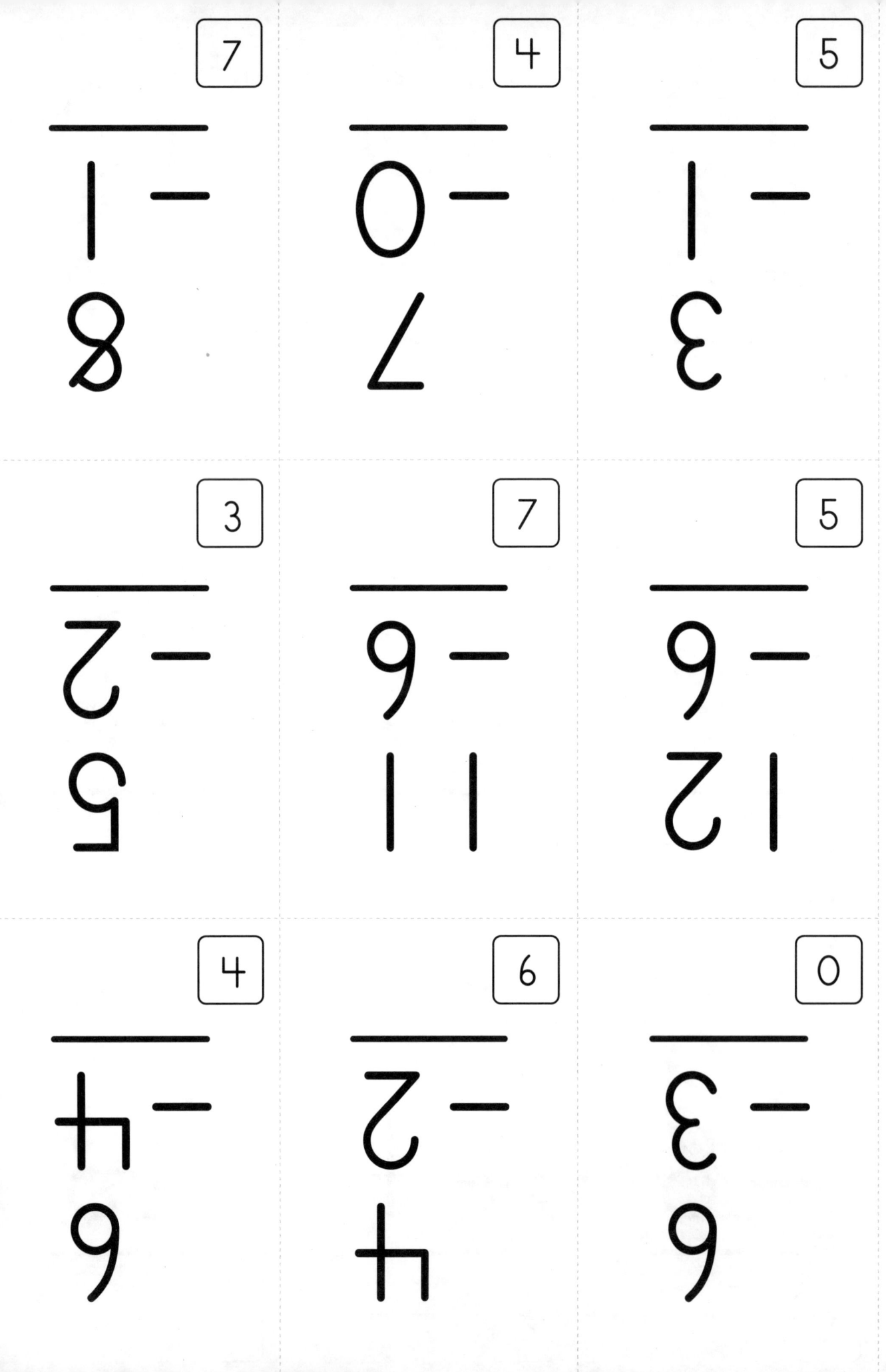